Contents

Watching planes

Have you ever watched planes landing
at an airport?   Do you remember
the deafening roar of the engines?

How do the planes know where to land?
And which way to go afterwards?

Can we land please?

This is the inside of the control tower at an airport.   The control tower is high so the controllers can see all of the airport.

Pilots talk to the controllers on their radios to ask permission to land.

9

Parking

Once on the ground, a plane taxis round the airport to its parking place.

The pilot needs help to stop in just the right place.   The ground crew are waiting.

Getting off

The ground crew push the steps
up to the door of the plane.
The passengers start to get off.

Have you ever travelled by plane?
Were the engines still running
when you got off?   Could you feel
the wind from the engines?

13

14

To the terminal

It's a long way from the plane to the terminal building. Do you think there will be a bus?

These passengers only have small bags to carry.   The rest of their baggage is still on the plane.

Collecting the baggage

Inside the terminal building there is another long walk to the baggage hall.

Can you see the baggage on the carousel? How do you think it got from the plane to the baggage hall?

Waiting . . .

More passengers are waiting to
get on to the empty planes.

First they must book their seats
at the check-in desk.   The computer
keeps a list.   Then they must hand in
their baggage.

19

More waiting . . .

Now the passengers must wait till
the planes are ready.   Perhaps they
will read books or look at the shops.

Where do you think the baggage is now?

21

At the planes

The ground crews are very busy.

The baggage arrives on a trolley.
Is this the right plane?
How can they be sure?

Loading the food is easy.
It goes straight into the kitchen.

A tanker drives up with the fuel.

Will they ever be ready?

23

Still waiting . . .

The passengers are still waiting.
They look at the departure board.

The departure board gives them
directions.   At last they can go.

Last-minute checks

While the passengers find their
seats, the pilot is in the cockpit
checking the controls.

In the control tower the radar
screen shows where other planes
are in the sky.

Cleared for take off

Finally, the control tower tells
the pilot that it is safe to take off.

The plane taxis to the end of
the take-off runway.   Then it turns
round, gathers speed and thunders
up into the sky.

28

29

Index